Minstrels 2
more medieval music to sing and play

selected and edited by
BRIAN SARGENT
Keswick Hall College of Education, Norwich

CAMBRIDGE UNIVERSITY PRESS

CAMBRIDGE

LONDON · NEW YORK · MELBOURNE

CAMBRIDGE UNIVERSITY PRESS
Cambridge, New York, Melbourne, Madrid, Cape Town,
Singapore, São Paulo, Delhi, Tokyo, Mexico City

Cambridge University Press
The Edinburgh Building, Cambridge CB2 8RU, UK

Published in the United States of America by Cambridge University Press, New York

www.cambridge.org
Information on this title: www.cambridge.org/9780521215510

© Cambridge University Press 1979

This publication is in copyright. Subject to statutory exception
and to the provisions of relevant collective licensing agreements,
no reproduction of any part may take place without the written
permission of Cambridge University Press.

First published 1979
Re-issued 2011

A catalogue record for this publication is available from the British Library

Library of Congress Catalogue Card Number: 78-9562

ISBN 978-0-521-21551-0 Paperback

Cambridge University Press has no responsibility for the persistence or
accuracy of URLs for external or third-party internet websites referred to in
this publication, and does not guarantee that any content on such websites is,
or will remain, accurate or appropriate.

Acknowledgements

Full source references to songs are given on pages 47 and 48. Sources of illustrations are listed on page 48. The author and publisher would like to thank all those there listed for permission to reproduce material in this book.

While every effort has been made to contact copyright holders, the publishers apologize if any material has been included without permission.

Performing and recording rights are reserved and are administered by the Performing Rights Society, The Mechanical Copyright Protection Society and the affiliated bodies throughout the world. Applications should be made to these bodies for a relevant licence. Failure to so apply constitutes a breach of copyright.

Contents

Introduction   4
  1   L'homme armé (The man at arms)   6

Two canonic pieces
  2   Salve mater misericordiae (Unto God)   8
  3   Si quis amat (Friend, help!)   9

A dance song
  4   Kalenda maya (No more delaying) by Raimbaut de Vaqueiras   10

Two Christmas songs
  5   Verbum patris (God's great plan)   12
  6   Verbum caro (Word of God)   14

Two English songs
  7   Me lykyth ever (The place I love)   15
  8   Westron wynde (Western wind)   16

A Latin song
  9   Festa dies agitur (Christmas time is here again!)   17

Two German songs
  10   Elslein, liebstes Elselein (Caroline, dear Caroline)   18
  11   Des soltu clein geniessen (The rotten cheeky devil!) by Konrad von Würzburg   19

Two songs by Guillaume de Machaut
  12   Douce dame jolie (I'm lost in adoration)   21
  13   Quant je sui mis (When I go my girl to see)   22

Two songs from Spain
  14   Como poden (Let us sing aloud)   23
  15   Ad mortem festinamus (As through life)   24

A trouvère song
  16   Ce fu en mai (I woke one day) by Moniot d'Arras   26

Two thirteenth-century motets
  17   Huic main (One bright morning)   27
  18   Hare, hare, hye! – Balaam! (Ah, my friend)   28

  19   Ave regina caelorum (All hail, gracious queen) by Guillaume Dufay   30
  20   Echo la primavera (See how the spring advances) by Francesco Landini   32
  21   An excerpt from the *Play of Herod*   33
  22   Samson, dux fortissime (Samson, judge victorious)   37
  23   Felix namque   40

Two instrumental dances
  24   Rompeltier   42
  25   Welscher tantz   44

Suggestions for further activities   46

Sources   47

Introduction

Interest in 'early music' has been growing steadily for many years, and it is now quite easy to hear performances and recordings of music ranging from plainsong to baroque cantatas and concertos at a very high standard of scholarship and interpretation. As such music becomes better known, more people feel the urge to sing and play it themselves, as well as just to listen.

Collections of easy and attractive early music, other than in expensive, scholarly editions, are relatively few, and this book, like its predecessors *Troubadours* and *Minstrels*, is designed to help increase the supply.

Texts If vocal pieces are to be more accessible, they must be given English texts in addition to the originals. Some people have problems enough in their own language, without having to grapple with those of medieval Europe. For those who are prepared to try, use of the original words will certainly give a better result than the English, not least because the languages such as Latin and *langue d'oc* lend themselves much more easily to the complex rhyme schemes of medieval poets. Some guidance in pronunciation is included though there is not space to deal with all the subtleties of medieval languages. The English texts, for which no literary merit is claimed, are offered simply for performance in situations which, for one reason or another, make the use of the original impracticable. If their subject, style or competence is unacceptable, users of the book are encouraged to write more suitable texts of their own.

Rhythm As the rhythm of many medieval songs is not clear from the notation a variety of interpretations is possible, ranging from the free speech rhythms of plainsong to the dance-like character implied by some troubadour songs. For example, the famous *rota*, *Sumer is icumen in* may be sung in either 6/8 or 4/4 time, beginning ♩ ♪♩ ♪or ♩ ♩ ♩ ♩ and other twelfth and thirteenth-century songs may be treated in the same way.

Pitch Scholars consider it unlikely that the 'middle c' of the clef in medieval manuscripts was of fixed pitch. They also believe that in those days pitches were only relative. Certainly a literal interpretation of the notes in such pieces would quite often result in a range unsuitable for most modern singers. Many of the melodies have therefore been transposed. Scholars who transcribe medieval tunes generally – and understandably – use the ♮ clef. However, the ordinary treble clef is used in this book because it indicates the pitch most often used in schools. The pitch at which the melody in its original state began is indicated by the C clef and the square black note(s) at the beginning of each piece. Where an accidental has been placed above rather than in front of its note, it does not appear in the original manuscript, but experts think it would have been played or sung thus.

Instrumentation In many cases the recorder, the guitar (used melodically or in open-fifth chords) and the glockenspiel may be the only suitable pitched instruments available.

portative organ   *hurdy-gurdy*   *nakers*   *bagpipe*

Musicians from the Luttrell Psalter. Fourteenth century.

Musicians from the fifteenth-century antiphoner in St Helen's Church, Ranworth.

However, even such restricted resources, imaginatively used, can give satisfying results. But nowadays makers of early instruments are working overtime, and exciting possibilities are opening up, not only in secondary schools. Unpitched percussion instruments – drum, tambour, tambourine, triangle and the rest – are generally easy to come by and, used with discrimination and restraint, can add much to the colour, vitality and variety of the music. Where the use of a drone is worth considering, a suggestion to that effect has been made. Care is needed, however, as the use of these features can easily become a habit and be overdone. In vocal pieces an instrumental introduction and an interlude between stanzas can, if desired, be fabricated from phrases of the melody.

Tempi and expression We need not suppose that 'early' musicians were indifferent to pace and dynamics just because they rarely left any indications. Satisfactory solutions should emerge from the use of critical experiment. The metronome marks are merely suggestions.

Conclusion As in so many fields of human activity, ignorance of a particular kind of music – especially medieval or contemporary – is its chief enemy. Once the suspicion and prejudice are broken down a whole new world of possibilities is opened up. For much early music still lies half-forgotten on library shelves and in museums; it may still be in manuscript and therefore available only through microfilm or photocopy. In rare cases it may even be still awaiting rediscovery. Although the amateur is unlikely to experience that satisfaction, if his interest and enthusiasm are strong enough the search can still be very rewarding.

1 *L'homme armé*

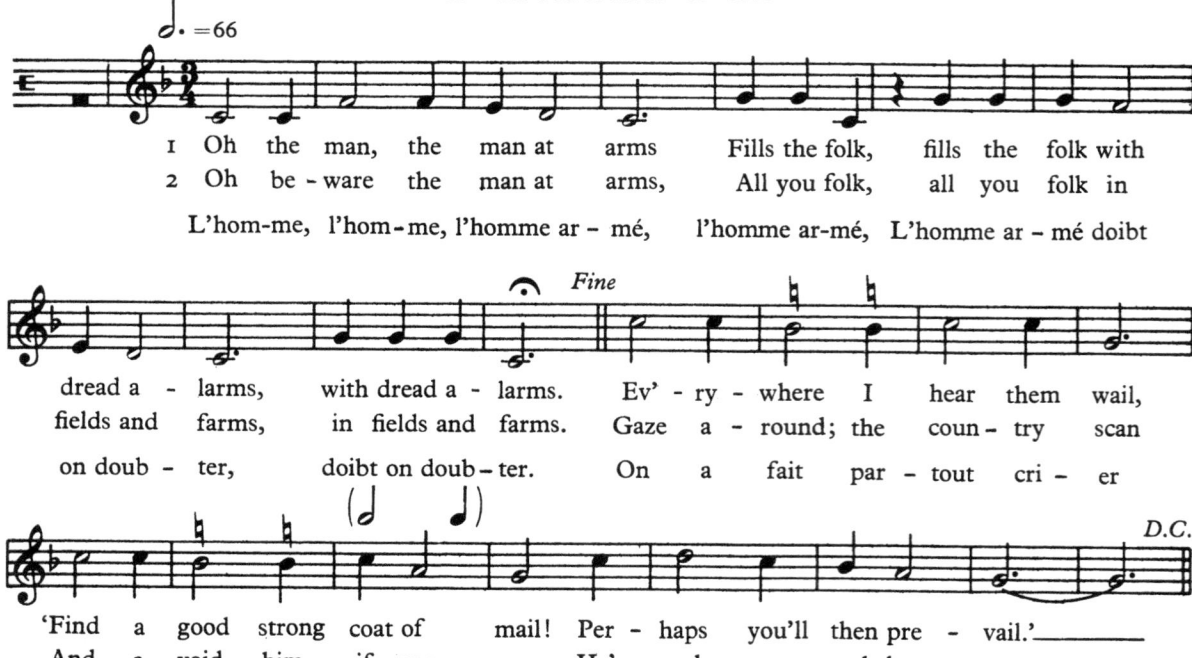

1. Oh the man, the man at arms Fills the folk, fills the folk with dread a-larms, with dread a-larms. Ev'-ry-where I hear them wail, 'Find a good strong coat of mail! Per-haps you'll then pre-vail.'

2. Oh be-ware the man at arms, All you folk, all you folk in fields and farms, in fields and farms. Gaze a-round; the coun-try scan And a-void him if you can. He's such a ruth-less man.

L'hom-me, l'hom-me, l'homme ar-mé, l'homme ar-mé, L'homme ar-mé doibt on doub-ter, doibt on doub-ter. On a fait par-tout cri-er Que chas-cun se viegne ar-mer D'un hau-bre-gon de fer.

3. Guard against all men at arms,
   But forget, but forget your foolish qualms,
      your foolish qualms.
   Bar the door and lock the gate,
   Waking early, watching late;
   Escape a dreadful fate.
   Guard against all men (etc.)

Optional drum part:

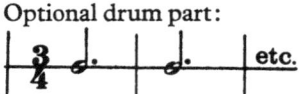

No-one is really sure where this famous tune originally came from. Most experts think it is probably an old folk song, though at least one scholar believed it to have been written by the Flemish–Burgundian composer Antoine Busnois (d.1492). Certainly the melody seems to date from the fifteenth century, and it was very popular with composers from Dufay (fifteenth century) to Carissimi (seventeenth), who used it as the basis for settings of the Mass. It was also treated in other ways, as the four-part version here shows. Robert Morton, an English composer, was attached to the Burgundian court from 1457 and died in 1475 or 1476. A number of his songs were popular all over Europe. His song *Il sera pour vous conbatu* is one of the first known compositions to incorporate the *L'homme armé* melody. He later altered it slightly and added a fourth part to make this consort version, set out here for recorders: descant, two trebles and tenor. It can be easily adapted for other combinations of instruments.

Medieval soldiers with flail and club.

Consort version by Robert Morton

2 Salve mater misericordiae

This is part of a *conductus* (processional song) of the same name dating from the second half of the thirteenth century. The manuscript was found in the binding of a book in the Bodleian Library, Oxford. Although this piece is a *rondellus*, in which all the voices start simultaneously at different points in the same melody, it may, as here, be sung as a round, each voice beginning in turn at the time intervals shown by the numbers. The first voice sings the first nine bars, repeats the first six and then follows arrow **A** to the last two. The second sings the first nine bars, repeats the first three and then follows arrow **B** to the last two. The third sings the whole eleven bars straight through without repeat. In the original version the entire piece was apparently sung to the one Latin word *Quae*. If you prefer a secular text to the sacred one provided, try the following.

Run and get a pail of water;
  Call your friends and neighbours too.
Smother the flames; shut the doors.
  Shout { out, / aloud, } 'Fire!'

3 Si quis amat

This round is rather unusual in that the second voice enters before the end of the first voice's first phrase. Apart from this, however, it works in the normal way. Singers end on the notes with pause marks which are of course to be observed only at the conclusion of the piece. The original text is a Latin homily in miniature: 'If anyone loves to slander by his words the life of those who are absent, let him know that this kind of course is unworthy of him.' Another text in lighter vein has been provided.

Singers round a lectern, from the Ranworth Antiphoner.

4 Kalenda maya

2   The day we're spending in sport contending,
    On foot and ball our strength expending.
    We're not intending to be offending
    With fight or brawl, our goal defending.
    Both great and small we love befriending;
    To short and tall we're condescending.
    Now bending and tending
    Our bruis'd limbs, home we're wending.
    Their mending is pending!
    And now our song is ending.

2   Dona grazida, quecx lauz'e crida
    vostra valor, qu'es abelhida;
    e qui·us oblida, pauc li val vida.
    Per qu'ie·us azor, don' eyssernida?
    Quar per gensor vos ai chauzida,
    e per melhor de pretz complida,
    blandida, servida,
    genses qu'Erecx Enida.
    Bastida fenida,
    n'Engles, ai l'estampida.

Although Raimbaut de Vaqueiras was a troubadour from Provence, which did not become a part of France until late in the fifteenth century, this song may be said to come from France for two reasons. The manuscript is now in the National Library in Paris, and an oft-quoted legend tells how Raimbaut at the court of Montferrat was asked to write words for a dance tune which was then being played by minstrels from northern France, *Kalenda maya* being the result. The melody itself is of a type called in France an *estampie* and in Provence an *estampida*. Raimbaut, who died in 1207, led a wandering life in France, Italy, Spain, Sicily, the Balkans and the Middle East. He was a faithful vassal to Boniface I, Marquis of Montferrat, took part in the Fourth Crusade and is thought to have lost his life in a battle against the Bulgarians. Thirty-five of his songs (seven with their melodies) have survived. *Kalenda maya* means the first of May.

Guide to pronunciation

-aya, as in maya, etc. = áhyah
-lh, as in auzelh = ell + yuh
chanz = kannts (not nasal)
que·m = kemm
  before a letter has the same function as an apostrophe in modern French.
pros = prohss (closed o)
cors = korss (open o)
gelos = jellóhss (closed vowel)
ans = annss
quecx = cakes
pauc = powk
eyssernida = essairnédda
Erecx = erréks

Dancers, from a fourteenth-century manuscript.

5 Verbum patris

♩=84

1. God's great plan is just be-gin-ning. O, O, All man-kind He aims at win-ning O, O, from the con-se-quence of sin-ning. This is then the plan. Ey, ey, e - ya, joy both near and far!
1. Ver - bum pa - tris hu - ma - na - tur, O, O, dum pu - el - la sa - lu - ta - tur, O, O, sa - lu - ta - ta fe - cun - da - tur vi - ri ne-sci - a. Ey, ey, e - ya, no - va gau-di - a!

2. Part the first is ex - e - cu-ted O, O, when a maid-en is sa - lu - ted, O, O,
2. No-vus mo - dus ge - ni - tu - rae, O, O, sed ex - ce - dens vim na - tu - rae, O, O,

4. Last, His life's in - spir-ing sto - ry O, O, and His cru - ci - fi - xion go - ry, O, O,
4. In pa - ren - te sal - va - to - ris, O, O, non est pa - rens no - stri mo - ris, O, O,

then con-ceives, al-though re-pu-ted not to have a man. Ey, - ey, - e - ya, joy both near and far!
dum u - ni - tur cre - a - tu - rae cre-ans om-ni - a. Ey, - ey, - e - ya, no-va gau-di - a!

crowned by resurrection's glory, faith's dull embers fan. Ey, - ey, - e - ya, joy both near and far!
vir-go pa-rit, nec pu-do-ris mar-cent li - li - a. Ey, - ey, - e - ya, no-va gau-di - a!

3. Next – and *this* is not a fable – O, O,
God's son's born within a stable O, O,
As a humble child, but able
Gulfs of sin to span. Ey, ey, …

Thus God's plan has its beginning. O, O,
Still mankind He aims at winning O, O,
From the consequence of sinning.
This is still the plan. Ey, ey, …

3. Audi partem praeter morem, O, O,
virgo parit salvatorem, O, O,
creatura creatorem,
patrem filia. Ey, ey, …

5. Homo Deus nobis datur, O, O,
datus nobis demonstratur, O, O,
dum pax terris nuntiatur,
caelis gloria. Ey, ey, …

Stanzas 3 and 5 are sung in unison to the tune of Stanza 1.

Though it has French characteristics this lively piece, containing dance elements, seems to be English, one of very few such survivors. Scholars disagree as to whether the three-part version dates from the twelfth century or the thirteenth, though the balance of opinion seems to favour the late twelfth.

Nativity scene from a fourteenth-century manuscript.

6 Verbum caro

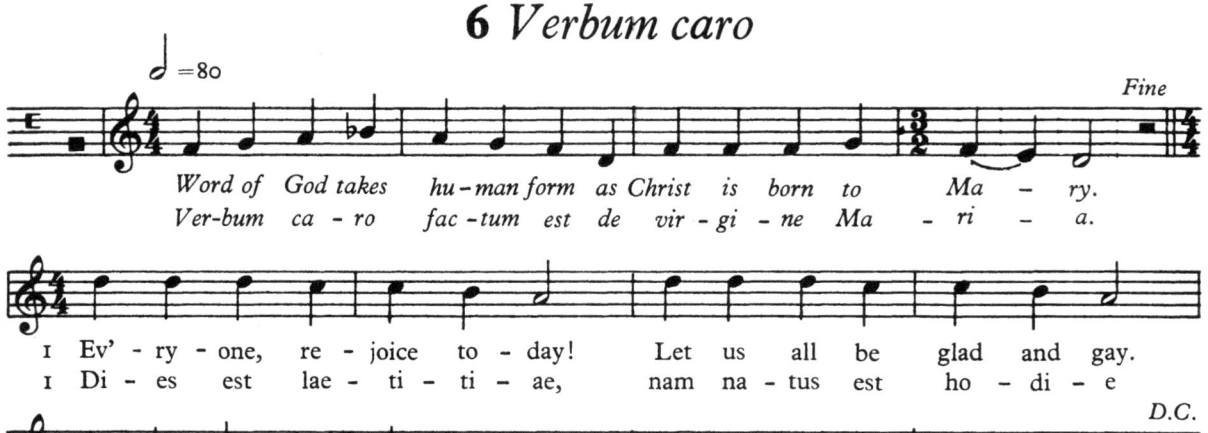

Word of God takes hu-man form as Christ is born to Ma - ry.
Ver-bum ca - ro fac-tum est de vir-gi - ne Ma - ri - a.

1 Ev'-ry-one, re-joice to-day! Let us all be glad and gay.
1 Di-es est lae-ti-ti-ae, nam na-tus est ho-di-e

Ce-le-brate in song and play, for Christ is born to Ma - ry.
fi-li-us de vir-gi-ne, de vir-gi-ne Ma - ri - a.

2 Peace has come to men at last;
All their fear of doom is past.
Satan's triumph is down cast
When Christ is born to Mary. *Word...*

3 Earth begins to fill with light
Through a girl who's pure and bright.
Evil spirits take their flight,
Now Christ is born to Mary. *Word...*

4 See, the door is open wide!
Cast all evil thoughts aside:
No more hatred, lust or pride
Since Christ is born to Mary. *Word...*

5 Angel choirs the shepherds told
That the child they'd soon behold
Would in kingly power unfold
As Christ, the son of Mary. *Word...*

6 Jesus, listen to our prayer!
Help us all your work to share.
Guard and guide us ev'rywhere,
O Christ, you son of Mary. *Word...*

2 O vos omnes psallite,
pace facta credite,
angelo nunciante
de virgine Maria. *Verbum...*

3 Lux venit de Lumine
in intacta virgine;
noe, noe dicite
de virgine Maria. *Verbum...*

4 Portam clausam graditur,
qui alcio genitur,
Deus homo nascitur
de virgine Maria. *Verbum...*

5 Fatur a pastoribus,
dum natus est parvulus
rex potens fortissimus,
de virgine Maria. *Verbum...*

6 O Jesu quem credimus,
da salutem omnibus
super in caelestibus
de virgine Maria. *Verbum...*

This is an anonymous carol from the fourteenth century. The Latin words of the *burden* ('Verbum caro factum est de virgine Maria') appear in a set of poems in the *Red Book of Ossory*, which was written by the Franciscan Richard de Ledrede, Bishop of Ossory in Ireland from 1317 to 1360, to supply edifying words for existing popular tunes.

7 Me lykyth ever

The fourteenth century and the early fifteenth have left few secular songs with English texts. This is one of a handful in an interesting manuscript in Cambridge University Library. It formerly belonged to Lord Howard de Walden and contains two-part and three-part songs in English, French and Latin, as well as Latin sermons, memoranda and other pieces of information.

The lower part of this song is almost certainly instrumental. The most suitable modern instrument is a bassoon (an octave lower), but the part may be played on 'cello, quiet trombone, viola, or even a B-flat clarinet reading a tone higher.

The following is a modernized version of the text:

> The place I love the deepest, the best,
> Is Winchester, that handsome city.
> The buildings are fine; you'd be impressed
> By the men, and my!, the girls are pretty.
> The air is good indoors and out;
> The city stands under a hill.
> The rivers flow all round about;
> The town is ruled with strength and skill.

Guide to pronunciation

lykyth = licketh
ys = is

8 Westron wynde

♩=80

We-stron wynd, when wyll thow blow, the smalle rayne downe can rayne? Cryst, yf my love were in my armys and I yn my bed a-gayne.

Here are three stanzas in modern English to fit this tune:

1. Western wind, when will you blow
   And bring the fine, soft rain?
   I wish my girl were in my arms
   And I back at home again!

2. Water stretches all around,
   But timbers warp and shrink.
   There's water everywhere I look,
   Yet never a drop to drink.

3. Western wind, come, strongly blow!
   Bring gentle, soothing rain,
   My girl to my embrace once more,
   And me to my home again.

There are two melodies of this name in existence. It is thought this one may well be a folk tune despite its unfolklike ending. There is a theory that although they do not fit together very well, the two tunes may both be voice parts of a lost song composed by Henry VIII when a youth. This is probably conjecture but there are several other pieces by Henry which resemble this tune. The other melody was used as the basis of Mass settings by the sixteenth-century composers Taverner, Tye and Shepherd (Sheppard).

Guide to pronunciation

wynde = wind as in winding
wyll = will
Cryst = Christ
yf = if
armys = arms
yn = in

9 Festa dies agitur

2 Evil's power begins to wane; *Sing aloud with might and main.*
Jesus Christ henceforth shall reign And Satan shall be put to flight.
Sing aloud with might and main, For vanquished are the powers of night.

3 Raise a grand triumphant strain; *Sing aloud with might and main.*
Broken is man's heavy chain; Salvation now appears in sight.
Sing aloud with might and main, For vanquished are the powers of night.

2 Gaudeamus igitur, *Mundo salus redditur*
In sole, qui dicitur Verus Deus in homine;
Mundo salus redditur, Christo nato de virgine.

3 O quam felix creditur, *Mundo salus redditur*
Mater, ad quam mittitur Vox de caelorum culmine;
Mundo salus redditur, Christo nato de virgine.

Although this little carol is found in a thirteenth-century manuscript in the British Library, the melody with its original secular text appears in the famous Montpellier Codex of southern France. It has no key signature, but it is quite possible that one was intended. Try the tune both ways. There is medieval precedent for providing an alternative text for a different season of the Church year. The English words may be used for either Christmas or Easter by varying the first word.

10 *Elslein, liebstes Elselein*

1. Ca-ro-line, dear Ca-ro-line, how far you are from me!
   Mo-rose and wretch-ed, here I pine; with you I long to be.

1. Els-lein, lieb-stes El-se-lein, wie gern wär ich bei dir!
   So sein zwei tie-fe Was-ser wohl zwi-schen dir und mir.

2 Thoughts like this inflict great strain
    on me, my distant dear.
    The stress will drive me quite insane
    while you are nowhere near.

3 Soon, I hope, my luck will change,
    and ev'rything be fine.
    Meantime my eager thoughts will range
    round you, my Caroline.

2 Das bringt mir grosse Schmerzen,
    herzallerliebster Gsell!
    Red ich von ganzem Herzen,
    habs für gross Ungefäll.

3 Hoff, Zeit werd es wohl enden,
    Hoff, Glück werd kommen drein,
    Sich in alls Guts verwenden,
    herzliebstes Elselein.

The Locheim, Schedel and Glogau song books are collections of German part music surviving from the latter half of the fifteenth century. This piece is from the Glogau book, by far the largest of the three, which contains 294 items, including Latin hymns, German songs and instrumental pieces. In this song the instrumental lines have been scored for violin and viola/two clarinets/two 'cellos/two bassoons, or any suitable combination of these.

11 *Des soltu clein geniessen*

Konrad von Würzburg is said to have been the first German poet–musician to support himself as an independent professional artist through performances and commissions. He was no aristocrat, but was born to middle-class parents between 1220 and 1230, and after living for a time in Strasbourg, settled in Basle, where he died in 1287. In his time Konrad was a notable and popular artist. He was a prolific writer, and his poetic output has been estimated at some 85,000 lines. The original three stanzas of this song describe the challenge flung at a rival whom the singer clearly holds in great disdain. The melody uses the notes of the Phrygian Mode, which you can find on the piano by playing an octave scale of white notes, starting on e.

Konrad von Würzburg dictating to a scribe.

Des soltu clein geniessen

2 Come landlord, join the party
   If you can stand the wretched dolt;
   His mental state's pathetically hazy.
   Be sociable and hearty,
   But lock the door and slip the bolt –
   The situation's absolutely crazy.
   He'll surely try to dodge humiliation,
   But I'm resolved to start his castigation
   And put an end to all this aggravation.

2 Wirt, ist diu tür beslossen?
   So ziuch mir doch die riegel für,
   Vil lieber wirt, daz er mir nit entrynne!
   Ich bin sîn unverdrossen,
   Die sîne kunst ich vil wol spür:
   Ô zarter got, wie gern wærę er von hynnen!
   Solt ich mich hie in kunst mit ym ergetzen,
   Mit mym gesange wil ich in hie letzen,
   Ich weiss, er müss sich hindern ofen setzen.

Guide to pronunciation, giving modern German equivalent

die (also hie, riegel, etc.) = die + e, as in Knabe
daz = das   hât: a is long
dym = dihm   ziuch: iu = üh
ûf: û is long   sîn ⎫ : i is long
heyss = heiss   sîne ⎭
sînr: i is long   wærę = wäre, final e is elided
ym = im   mym = mihm

12 Douce dame jolie

3A This chronic agitation creates such palpitation
   that, brought to sheer prostration, quite exhausted here I lie.

4B I'm stunned by deprivation. Deflation induces me to sigh.
   I'm stung by provocation. Vexation turns all my thoughts awry.

5A I must have ventilation! The threat of suffocation,
   complete asphyxiation, I'm unable to defy.

6B Must look for relaxation. Migration could help me by and by
   forget my perturbation. Starvation will loom if I don't try!

7A Is hoped-for delectation in rapturous elation
   just vain imagination? For if so, I'd rather die!

Douce dame jolie is by Guillaume de Machaut (see page 22). Its structure as sung in full is as follows:

1A/2B/3A/1A/1A/4B/5A/1A/1A/6B/7A/1A

Guide to pronunciation

mie = mée-yuh
seur = sirr
moy = mwěh
fors = forr (open o)
Qu'ades = kadéss (open a)
chierie = sherry + yuh
ay = eh (pure vowel, closed)

13 Quant je sui mis

1 When I go my girl to see, wild-ly pal-pi-tat-ing,
   o-ver-flows my heart with glee; she's in-to-xi-cat-ing! Yes! I'm sure
   I can make her love me. Hope's ex-hi-la-rat-ing!

1 Quant je sui mis au retour de veoir ma dame,
   il n'est peinne ne dolour que j'aie, par m'ame. Dieus! C'est drois
   que je l'aim, sans blame, de loial amour.

2 Gorgeous, gay and bright is she, vastly scintillating.
    From her toils I can't get free; she's just fascinating!
    Still, perhaps I can make her love me. Doubt's exasperating!

3 Anxious I've begun to be, glumly speculating,
    tortured to the third degree, for her answer waiting.
    No! She may never come to love me. Fear's excruciating!

2 Sa biauté, sa grant douçour d'amoureuse flame,
    par souvenir, nuit et jour, m'esprent et enflame.
    Dieus! C'est drois que je l'aim, sans blame, de loial amour.

3 Et quant sa haute valour mon fin cuer entame,
    servir la weil sans folour penser ne diffame.
    Dieus! C'est drois que je l'aim, sans blame, de loial amour.

Guillaume de Machaut had a busy career as king's secretary, lay canon and poet, but he also found time to write the music which has made him the most famous composer of the fourteenth century. As well as a fine setting of the Mass and many three-part and four-part songs Machaut composed a number of monophonic (tune only) pieces, including these short, simple *virelais* with their jaunty rhythm.

Quant je sui mis is in fact a *virelai* in name only, as it is not written in the standard *virelai* form (AbbaA).

Guide to pronunciation

veoir = vwair
weil = vwell + yuh

Dame Nature presenting her children to Guillaume de Machaut.

14 *Como poden*

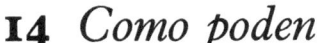

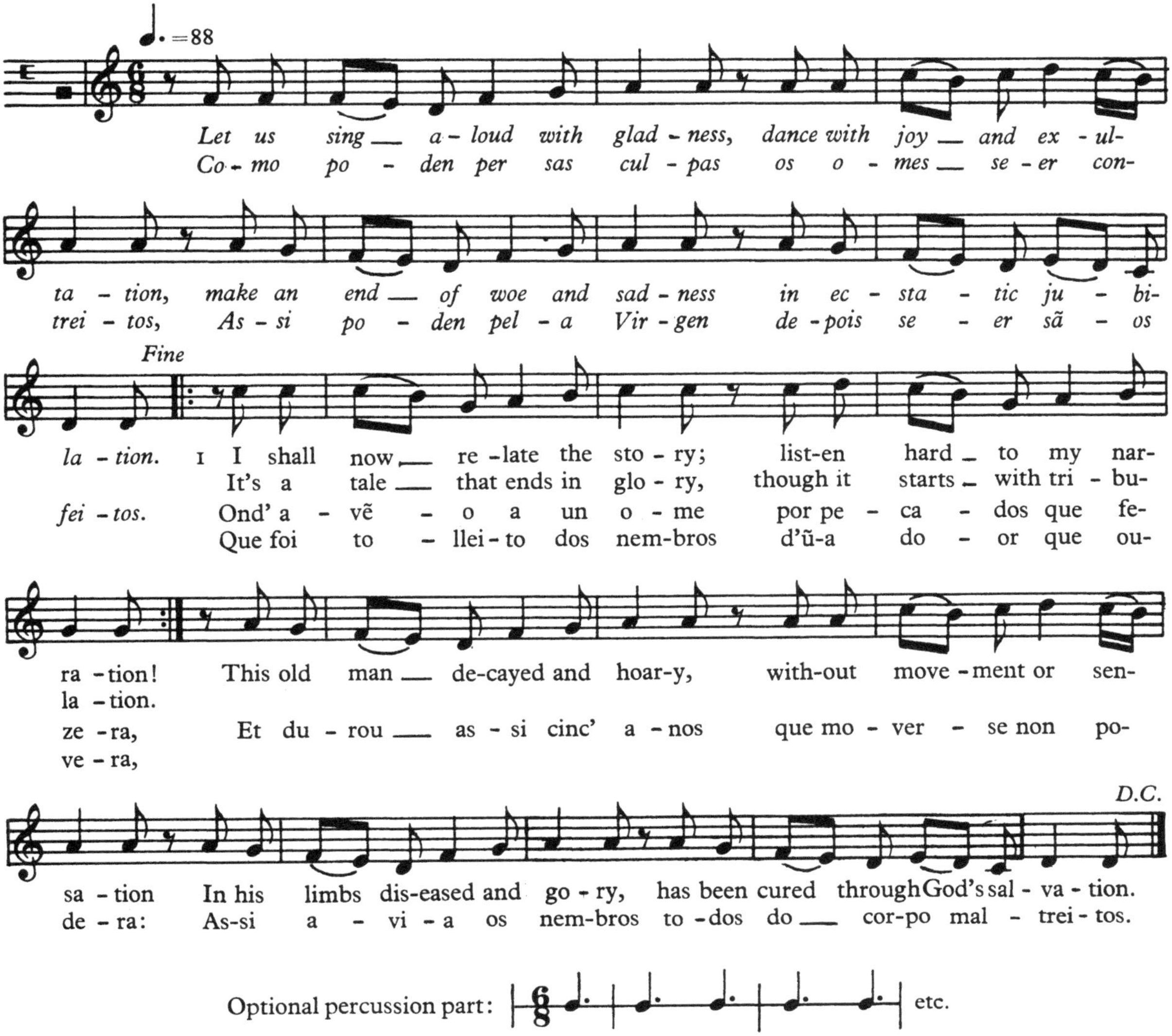
♩. = 88
Let us sing a - loud with glad - ness, dance with joy and ex - ul-
Co - mo po - den per sas cul - pas os o - mes se - er con-
ta - tion, make an end of woe and sad - ness in ec - sta - tic ju - bi-
trei - tos, As - si po - den pel - a Vir - gen de - pois se - er sã - os
Fine
la - tion. 1 I shall now re - late the sto - ry; list-en hard to my nar-
It's a tale that ends in glo - ry, though it starts with tri - bu-
fei - tos. Ond' a - vẽ - o a un o - me por pe - ca - dos que fe-
Que foi to - llei - to dos nem-bros d'ũ-a do - or que ou-
ra - tion! This old man de-cayed and hoar-y, with-out move - ment or sen-
la - tion.
ze - ra, Et du - rou as - si cinc' a - nos que mo - ver - se non po-
ve - ra,
D.C.
sa - tion In his limbs dis-eased and go - ry, has been cured through God's sal - va - tion.
de - ra: As-si a - vi - a os nem-bros to - dos do cor-po mal - trei - tos.
Optional percussion part:
etc.

2 Never more the ruthless rigour
  of that cruel mutilation
Shall embitter and disfigure
  both his life and his vocation.
Now his strength's returned with vigour
  through this blest rejuvenation,
And his faith has grown much bigger
  since his thrilling restoration.

Guide to pronunciation

seer = say-air
sãos = sã-os
avẽo : v = b as Spanish
depois = dĕ-poys
fezera : z as in zest
d'ũa = d'oo-a
door = dŏ-or
durou = do-rue
cinc' = sink

During the latter half of the thirteenth century the Spanish kingdoms of Castile and Leon were ruled by King Alfonso X, who was known as *el Sabio* ('the Wise'). A cultured and enlightened monarch, he patronized troubadours and compiled the great collection of songs in honour of the Virgin Mary, *Las Cantigas de Santa Maria*, with texts in Galician–Portuguese dialect. This song is one of them.

15 Ad mortem festinamus

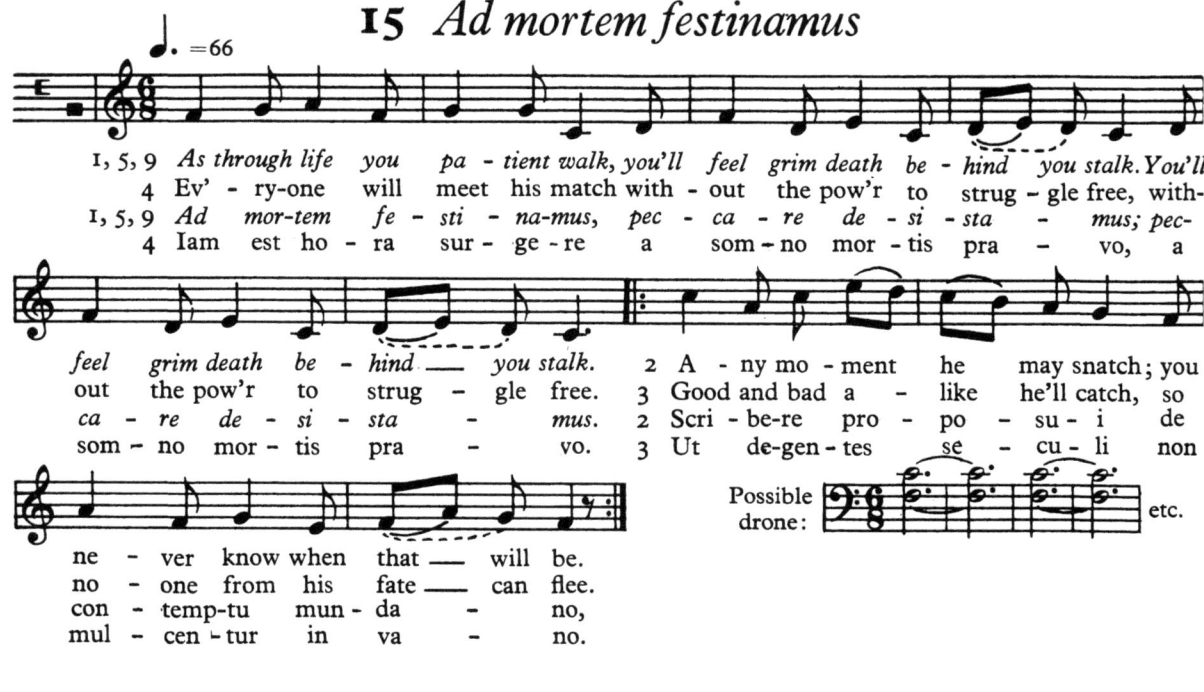

6 Gentle Mary, blessèd one, acknowledge our despairing cry!

7 Mindful of your holy Son, console us all, who have to die,

8 For until our course is run, we must on faith and hope rely. We must on faith and hope rely.

6 Alma virgo virginum in celis coronata,

7 Apud tuum filium sis nobis advocata,

8 Et post hoc exilium occurrens mediata, occurrens mediata.

Sing 8 to the music of 1, and 6 and 7 to the music of 2.

The fourteenth century saw more than its fair share of disaster and suffering. Its catastrophes included the Hundred Years War, civil strife, peasant rebellions, famines and, perhaps worst of all, the plague called the Black Death, which killed about a third of the population of Europe and left many of its survivors in a pitiable condition. Food and labour were scarce, and life was so uncertain that people could do little more than live from day to day. The prevailing outlook was 'Let us eat and drink; for tomorrow we die.'

This 'Dance of Death', which in form resembles the French *virelai*, comes from the *Llibre Vermell* ('Red Book'), a fourteenth-century manuscript in the famous mountain monastery of Montserrat near Barcelona in Catalonia.

The 7.7. metre of the Latin text does not lend itself easily to smoothly flowing English, and 7.8. has therefore been used. But if you prefer to keep 7.7. for the English too, try the following modifications.

You'll feel behind you death stalk.
You can't know when it will be.
So none can from his fate flee.
Without the pow'r to win free.

Acknowledge our distressed cry!
Console us all, who'll soon die,
On faith alone we rely.

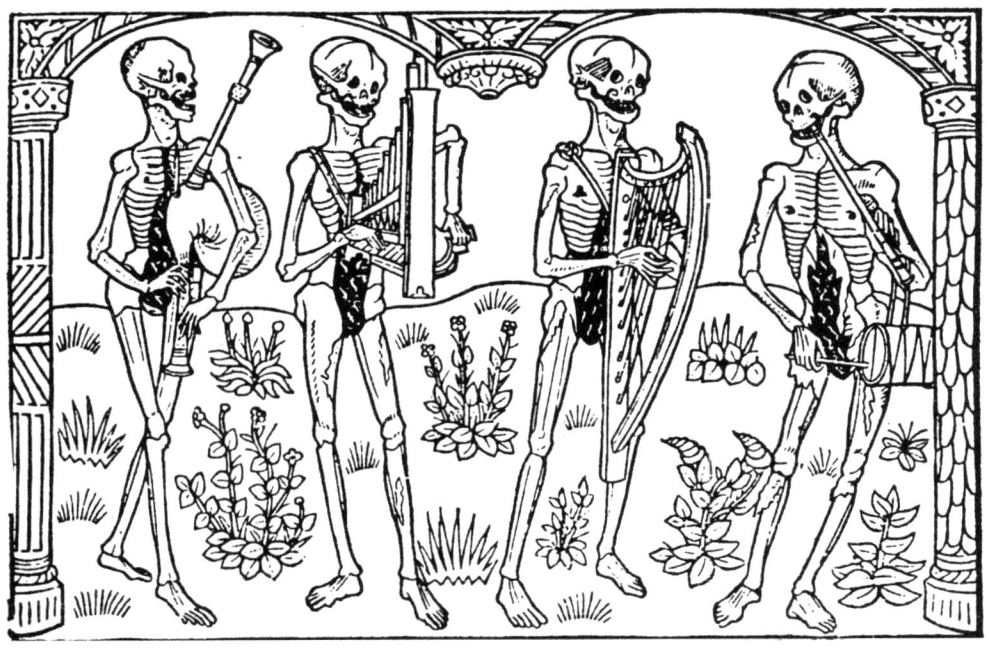

The theme of death in the midst of life continued to be popular in medieval illustrations. This woodcut of musician-skeletons comes from Guyot Marchand's 'Danse macabre' (1486).

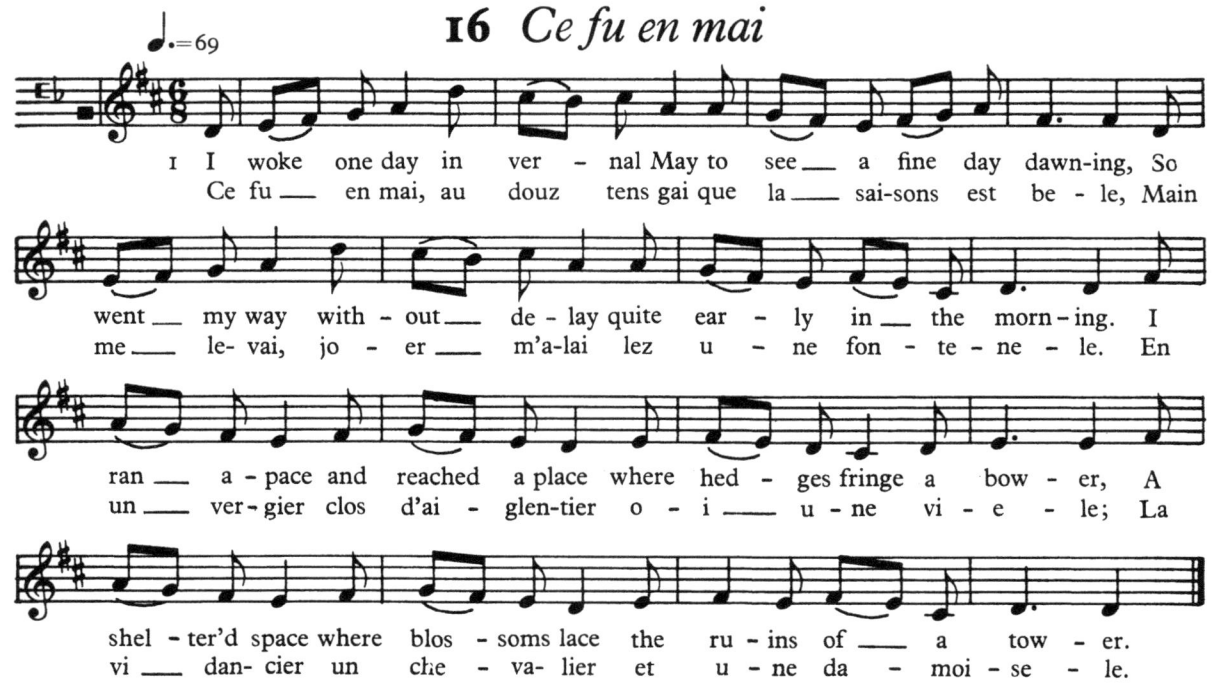

2 A little brook ran through the nook, whence came a sound entrancing,
   And so I took a cautious look, and saw a couple dancing.
   Within the glade a minstrel played a dance tune for their pleasure,
   And in the shade the knight and maid trod out a lively measure.

3 With nod and smile they danced a while, until they fell to talking
   In volatile and lively style, and off they started walking.
   Behind a screen of vivid green, well hid from observation,
   I watched the scene with mind serene and pensive admiration.

Arras, capital of the old French province of Artois (now called Pas de Calais), is the town which later became famous for its tapestry, and as such gave its name to the English language as a word for tapestry. Well-known examples occur in Shakespeare's *Hamlet* (III, 4), *King Henry IV*, Part I (II, 4) and *Merry Wives of Windsor* (III, 3).

Perron, Moniot d'Arras was born about 1190, and as a young man seems to have been a monk in the monastery of St Vedast in Arras (Vedast was Bishop of Arras in the sixth century). Moniot, who lived until after 1239, is regarded as one of the most important trouvères of his time. Eighty of his songs have survived with both words and music intact. The melody of this song is quoted in Hindemith's ballet *Nobilissima visione* (1938).

Guide to pronunciation

douz = as English dotes
tens = tanns (slightly nasal)
lez = lates
oi = o-ée (o very open)

17 Huic main

This secular motet comes from the great Montpellier manuscript. The lower part is derived from the first fifteen notes of *Haec dies*, a piece of Gregorian chant called a *gradual* and sung from the steps of the church altar. *Haec* (or *Hec*) *dies quam fecit Dominus* is Latin for 'This is the day the Lord has made.' You may notice that the long notes of the lower part have been formed into repeating groups of eight (with one seven near the end), making the pattern a a a b a. Over the top some unknown 'composer' has fitted a tune set to a simple pastoral text in French.

The instrumental lower part may be played on bells or organ, wind or string instrument. The upper part may be either sung or played – or both.

Guide to pronunciation

doz = as English dotes
coillant = kwellyánn (slightly nasal)
ja: soft j as modern French
qar = karr

18 Hare, hare, hye! — Balaam!

♩. = 76

Ah, my friend, hel - lo there! Are you rea - dy for the par - ty?
ner - vous girls es - cort - ed. Keep your tem - per much more stea - dy!
Ha - re, ha - re, hy - e! Goud - a - lier ont fet ou - an d'Ar-
que chas - cuns en - ba - le, que en sont En - glis - e - men quant

Please don't go! Ev' - ry - thing has been made rea - dy;
aren't you stay - ing? Ev' - ry - one is bright and heart - y,
Ba - la - am! Goud - a - lier ont bien (Ou! An!) leurs
Saint An - dri - e! Ha - re, ha - re gou - de - man et

By its chime this short rhyme
for a prime drink sub - lime.

Hear the min - strels play - ing; See the boo - zers sway - ing, maud - lin bal - lads
Why've you gone and snort - ed, ca - ter - ers ex -
ras E - sco - te - ri - e. Ca - ri - ta - te cri - e por Sain - te Ma -
il l'ont bien es - ta - le, E - le m'est trop

thugs have been de - port - ed, an - gri - ly re - tort - ed and all my words dis -
wit and fun dis - play - ing. I, the scene sur -
tens por la goud - a - le de - mi lot a mail - le por ce il font leur
ha - re dru - e - ri - e! Ho - nie soit tel

sets the time this short rhyme sets the
By its chime

bray - ing, all cour - te - sy mis - lay - ing and prim young girls dis - may - ing.
hort - ed and cakes from town trans - port - ed. Guests will have ca -
ri - e! Fai - tez moi de - mi - e de pou - mon et de fy - e.
ma - le qu'en mes ge - nous m'a - va - le: mer - veille ai que

tort - ed? Fine wines have been im - port - ed, scru - pu - lous - ly sort - ed,
vey - ing, ask who'll do the pay - ing, such a cost de -
tail - le. Si di - ent: 'Bien le vail - le!' Pas - si - ons l'as - sail - le!
vi - e! Mais bon vin sor - li - e ne mes - pris je

time for a prime drink sub - lime.
chime this short rhyme sets the

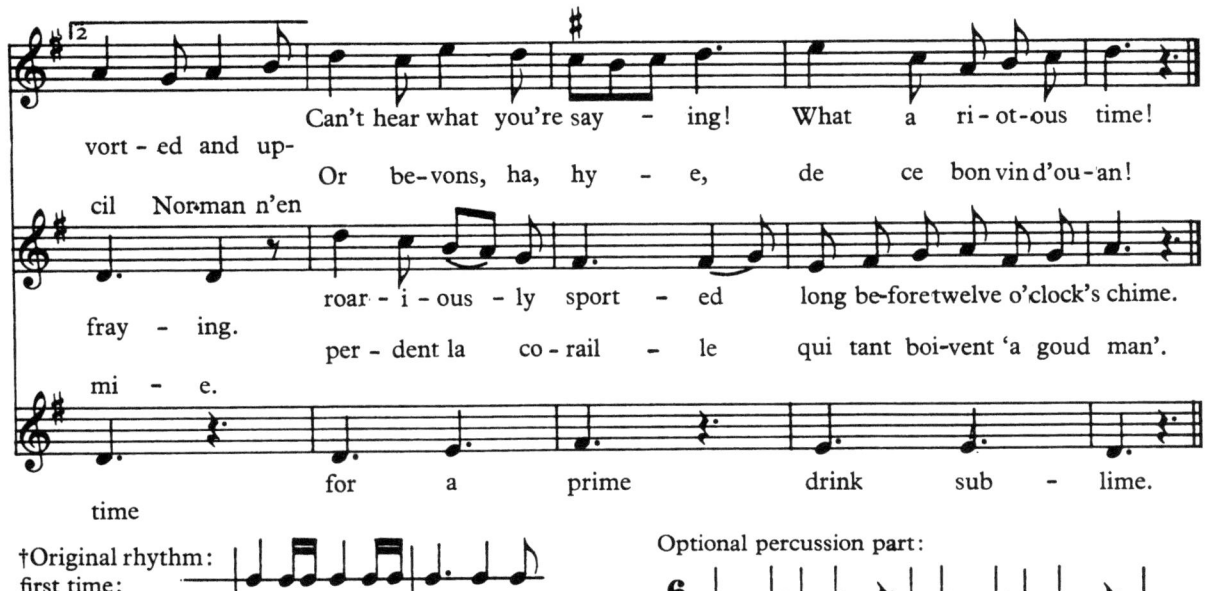

†Original rhythm:
first time:
second time as in song

Optional percussion part: etc.

Whether we like it or not, drinking and the composing of drinking songs have been part of human life since at least the early days of recorded history. Although we tend to think of motets as sacred, many thirteenth-century examples are, like this one, blatantly secular. *Hare, hare, hye!*, which was popular among students of the University of Paris, is a double motet, that is, with two different but simultaneous texts, in this case both in French. The tenor (lowest) part has no text in the original and is probably instrumental. Notice that the technique of voice exchange is used in the repeated sections. On reaching an asterisk for the first time each of the two upper voices changes places with the other for the second line of the words, reverting to its original stave at the end of the repeated section.

In medieval times the Biblical prophet Balaam was sometimes regarded as a comic, and even an intoxicated, character. Read about his ass and his trance in *Numbers* 22:20–35 and 24:15–19.

Guide to pronunciation

hare = há-ruh
ouan = o-wánn (slightly nasal)
fye = fée-yuh
lie = lée-yuh
chascuns = shahkewnss
lot: pronounce t

An illustration from a drinking song in a fifteenth-century English manuscript.

19 Ave regina caelorum

The Burgundian Guillaume Dufay, who died in 1474, was one of the greatest composers of the fifteenth century. The music he composed in his long life straddled the late medieval and early renaissance styles. This early motet, a setting of the Marian antiphon (short piece in praise of Mary sung before and after a psalm) *Ave regina caelorum*, was probably composed in the 1420s, and still shows some medieval characteristics. Notice the strings of 'sixth chords' (first inversions), the way the parts cross and re-cross, and the occasional 6/8 rhythms in individual voice parts. The accidentals above the notes are merely suggestions. The piece should not be sung too slowly.

A miniature of Guillaume Dufay and Gilles Binchois

20 Echo la primavera

♩. = 54

1, 5 See how the spring ad-van-ces and gives us all a to-nic! Best
4 Now is the time for glad-ness; our voi-ces min-gle sweet-ly. So
1, 5 E - cho la pri - ma - ve-ra che'l cor fa ral - le - gra-re, ten
4 L'er - be con gran fres - che-ça e fior' co-pro-no i pra-ti, e

time for songs and dan-ces, end of win-ter de - mo-nic. 2 Bright is the
bid fare-well to sad-ness; spring now rules us com-plete-ly. 3 Clear is the
p'è d'an-na-mo - ra - re e star con lie - ta ce - ra. 2 No' ve-giam
gli al-be-ri a-dor - na - ti so-no in si - mil ma - ne - ra. 3 In que-sto

sun - light glow - - ing; ev'ry-where birds are sing-ing.
wa - ter flow - - ing; ev'ry-where shoots are spring-ing.
l'a - ria e'l ten - - po che pur chiam' al - - le - gre-ça.
va - go tem - - po o - gni co - sa a va - ghe-ça.

Landini, the outstanding composer of fourteenth-century Italy and Machaut's rival as the greatest of the century, was a Florentine. Blind from early childhood, he nevertheless became famed as poet, philosopher, astrologer, organist, flautist and lutenist. Of his 154 extant compositions, some 141 are in the form of the *ballata*, the most popular type of Italian music of the time, with the structure A b b a A. This lively piece – incidentally his shortest – is one of them. The optional accidentals above the notes are *editor's* conjecture.

Guide to pronunciation
che = k
cera = thera
gli = l'yee

Francesco Landini

21 An excerpt from the *Play of Herod*

The *Play of Herod* (*Ordo ad representandum Herodem*) is one of ten church music dramas in a manuscript of the twelfth or thirteenth century called the *Fleury Play-book*. This book originally belonged to the Monastery of St Benoît-sur-Loire at Fleury and is now in the municipal library at Orléans. The complete *Play of Herod* represents the arrival of the Magi (or Kings), their encounter with Herod, their discovery and adoration of the baby Jesus, their dream and subsequent departure, and the murder of the Bethlehem children.

The fragments given here provide, as it were, bare bones which may be clothed with action and dialogue or mime to create a complete episode in the Biblical narrative of the Magi as recorded in Matthew 2.

If further instrumental music is needed for interludes, this may be easily derived from the existing vocal pieces. The order of the latter may of course be changed if you wish. The episode may be lengthened by performing the vocal pieces twice, the first time on instrument(s) alone, but this is not advisable in every case as it can reduce the pace and impact of the action.

Helpful notes on the history, text, music and production of this play may be found in the editions mentioned in Sources 21 on page 48.

Here is a possible plan of performance:

Order of performance	Section	Scenario	Performers
1	A	Entry of the Magi and attendants	Instruments only
2	A	Procession of the Magi and attendants	Stanza 1: the three Magi in unison and instruments
3	B	Procession halts. The Magi admire the star	The three Magi
4	G	Encounter with Herod (optional)	Instruments only
5	C	The Magi hail the star	The three Magi
6	D	They sing in joy as it leads them to the stable	The three Magi in unison or all voices
7	E	Procession to the stable	All voices and instruments
8	F	In the stable	The three Magi
9	G	The presentation of the gifts	The three Magi
10	B	Dream of the Magi (optional)	Instruments only
11	A	Withdrawal of the Magi and attendants	Stanza 2: all voices and instruments
12	A	Exit of the Magi and attendants	Instruments only

Characters

Singing parts: Caspar, Melchior, Balthasar — these may be sung by solo voices or groups

Attendants: Chorus

Speaking or miming parts: Herod, Attendants, Mary, Joseph, Angel

The Magi at the court of Herod, from a sixteenth-century painting by Hubert Cailleau.

Play of Herod

Section A (1, 2, 11, 12)

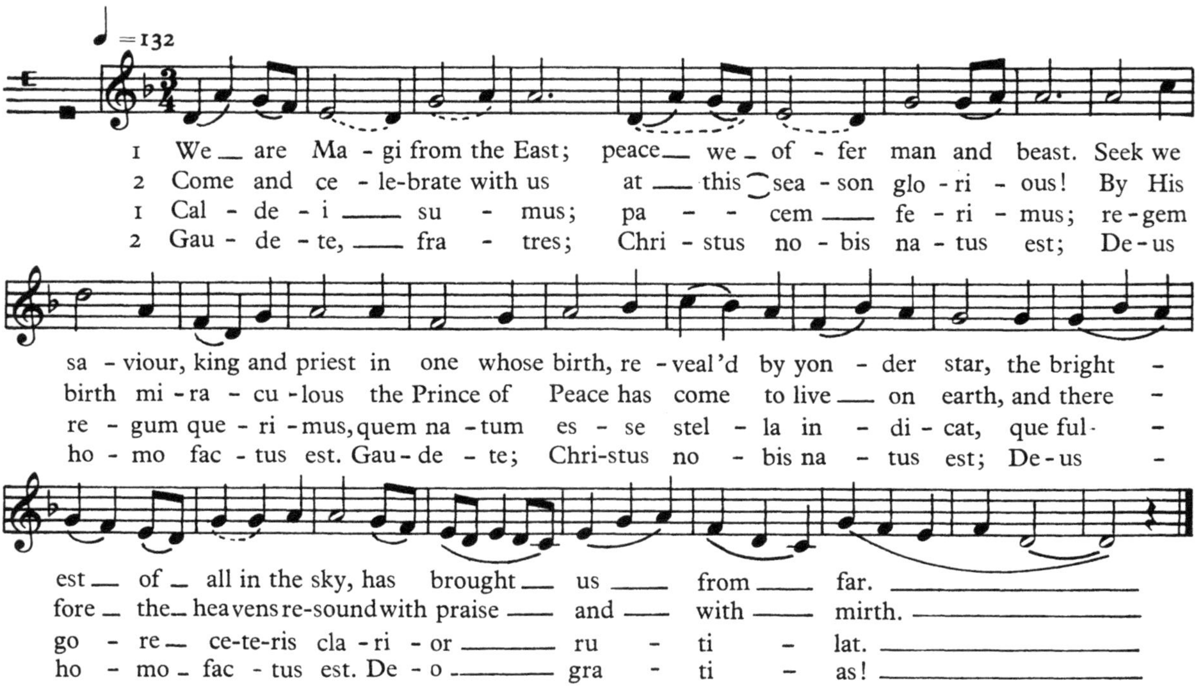

♩ = 132

1. We are Magi from the East; peace we offer man and beast. Seek we
2. Come and celebrate with us at this season glorious! By His
1. Caldei sumus; pacem ferimus; regem
2. Gaudete, fratres; Christus nobis natus est; Deus

saviour, king and priest in one whose birth, reveal'd by yonder star, the brightest of all in the sky, has brought us from far.
birth miraculous the Prince of Peace has come to live on earth, and therefore the heavens re-sound with praise and with mirth.
regum querimus, quem natum esse stella indicat, que fulgore ceteris clarior rutilat.
homo factus est. Gaudete; Christus nobis natus est; Deus homo factus est. Deo gratias!

Section B (3, 10)

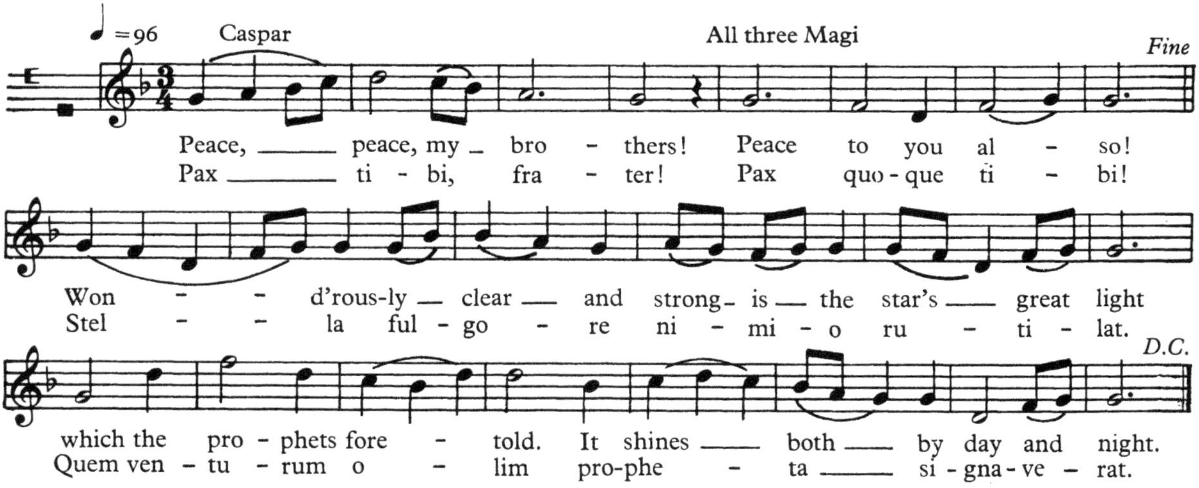

♩ = 96   Caspar   All three Magi   *Fine*

Peace, peace, my brothers! Peace to you also!
Pax tibi, frater! Pax quoque tibi!

Won - d'rously clear and strong is the star's great light
Stel - la fulgore nimio rutilat.

D.C.

which the prophets foretold. It shines both by day and night.
Quem venturum olim propheta signaverat.

Section C (5)

Caspar   Melchior   Balthasar

Star of glory! Star of mys't'ry! Star foretelling sacrifice!
Ecce stella! Ecce stella! Ecce stella (splendida)!

†Second time a semitone higher in the manuscript.

23 Felix namque

This is one of the earliest surviving pieces of church organ music. It dates from about 1400, and like much music of the time is based on a fragment of plainsong melody in long notes, taken in this case from an offertory which begins with the words 'Felix namque es' (Latin, meaning 'For thou art blessed'). The notes in brackets have been supplied by an editor, as the original manuscript lacks notes at those points.

Here the piece is arranged so that it may be played on any of the following instruments:

1. Keyboard: top stave and either line of the middle stave.
2. Descant recorder: top stave, and tenor recorder: upper line of bottom stave.
3. Clarinet (transposing), flute, oboe or violin: top stave and *either* clarinet (transposing), violin or viola: lower line of bottom stave *or* trombone, bassoon or 'cello: either line of middle stave.

24 Rompeltier

Thurston Dart called this piece 'a lively consort setting of a lively German folk song', but there is no text in the source of this instrumental version, which is sometimes attributed to the Netherlandish composer Jacob Obrecht (c. 1450–1505). The title seems to suggest a stamping dance. The piece may be played as it stands on A: descant, B: treble or descant, C: treble and D: tenor recorders, or an octave lower on A: flute, oboe or violin, B: the same (using the lower line), C: violin, viola or clarinet (transposing) and D: bassoon, 'cello or clarinet (transposing). In this case, C and D only should be transposed down an octave.

Peasants dancing. A copperplate engraving by Albrecht Dürer. 1514.

25 Welscher tantz

Optional percussion part: | $\frac{2}{2}$ ♩ ♫ ♩ ♩ | ♩ ♫ ♩ ♩ | etc., and | $\frac{3}{4}$ ♩ ♩ ♫ | ♩ ♩ ♫ | etc.

About the middle of the sixteenth century Wolfgang Küffer of Regensburg (Ratisbon), who studied at Wittenberg and Heidelberg, compiled a manuscript volume of 314 mixed Latin, German, French and Italian vocal and instrumental pieces. This anonymous dance, rather unusually in three and not four parts, is number 177. It is most effective when taken quickly. The title is unlikely to mean 'Welsh dance'. It may refer to the area now covered by southern France and northern Italy.

Dancers at a wedding, from a late fifteenth-century French manuscript.

Suggestions for further activities

The items listed below are supplementary to the full lists of collections of music, background reading, reference books and records which appear in the earlier books in this series, *Minstrels* and *Troubadours*.

Collections of music

Burnett, Michael, *A feast of music*, Chappell, 1976.

Seven simple medieval pieces have here been collected and arranged for use in the classroom. The music is scored for recorders and pitched and unpitched percussion, but Mr Burnett makes it clear that any suitable instruments may be used. Parts are provided in addition to the score. The pieces have been extensively edited and most have had their names changed, perhaps with a view to giving encouragement and confidence to teachers. The original titles and texts are not given, but for four of the pieces English words are provided.

McGrady, Richard J. (arr.), *Four thirteenth-century pieces*, Chester Recorder Series, no. 6, J. & W. Chester Ltd, 1973.

There are two well-known motets, a *clausula* and a *ductia* in this collection, all taken from the *Historical anthology of music*. Two of the pieces call for two descant recorders and one treble, one for descant, treble (or two trebles) and tenor, and the fourth for two descants, treble and tenor. Dr McGrady has transposed two of the pieces, written in two additional parts for the two-part *ductia*, and added some expression marks. He has also provided optional parts for percussion and 'cello. Technically the pieces are not difficult.

Marr, Peter (ed.), *Four medieval pieces* (for organ), Peters, 1972.

The four consist of two *estampies*, and two pieces of liturgical polyphony which are keyboard versions, one – incomplete – of a Marian hymn, and the other of an offertory. Three of the items are from the so-called Robertsbridge manuscript. Played in full the *estampies* are of quite substantial length, but they may be conveniently shortened by cutting out certain sections or *puncti*. The pieces may be played on the organ with only one stop – or on the clavichord. A useful collection, and a pleasant change from *Gems for the harmonium*.

Marrocco, W. Thomas, and Sandon, Nicholas, *Medieval music*, Oxford University Press, 1977.

To those in search of a truly comprehensive anthology this sumptuous collection is well worth its price. It contains 106 pieces ranging in date from the sixth century to the fifteenth, and divided into five categories: Sacred and Secular Monophony, Ars Antiqua, Ars Nova and the Fifteenth Century. Each item is provided with a historical note and, where appropriate, a translation of the text. Particularly interesting are a complete plainsong mass from Salisbury, together with rubrics and a plan of the Cathedral, and the Fleury *Play of Herod* in its entirety.

Parrish, Carl, and Ohl, John F., *Masterpieces of music before 1750*, Faber, 1952.
Parrish, Carl, *A treasury of early music*, Faber, 1959.

These two well-known anthologies in book form provide an invaluable conspectus of musical developments from plainchant to the mid-eighteenth century. Each *genre* is represented by one piece which is printed in full, prefaced by a descriptive paragraph. Problems of turnover make the books difficult for instrumentalists to use, but for a living study of the history of music they are otherwise admirable.

Stevens, Denis, *The treasury of English church music* vol. 1: *1100–1545*, Blandford, 1965.

For those wishing to take early English church music seriously this substantial, though not unduly expensive, volume of approximately quarto size and over 200 pages provides an excellent selection. There are 37 pieces in all; some, such as *Angelus ad virginem* and the sacred version of *Sumer is icumen in*, are well known and not difficult. Others, a five-part Magnificat by Fayrfax and a mass movement by Taverner for example, are decidedly challenging.

Tischler, Hans, *A medieval motet book*, Associated Music Publishers/Schirmer, 1973.

This is a collection of 18 thirteenth-century motets in a total of 30 versions 'compiled and edited for study and modern performance'. The editor provides a historical introduction, notes on each piece and English texts as well as the originals. Although a rather specialized publication it is warmly recommended to those interested in practical exploration of the rich but neglected repertory of the thirteenth-century motet.

Trowell, Brian (ed.), *Invitation to medieval music 3* and *4*, Stainer and Bell, 1976 and 1978.

For a more detailed survey of early music suitable for school use the reader is referred to *Music education review: a handbook for music teachers*, edited by Michael Burnett (Chappell, 1977).

Series

Antico Edition

A finely produced series of publications, edited for practical use by leading scholars. The pieces are for the most part taken from the late middle ages and the renaissance. Though few are easy, all are rewarding when attempted with competence and determination.

Musica sacra et profana

This American edition, which is handled in England by Breitkopf & Härtel (London) Ltd, consists of nearly 100 publications of medieval, renaissance and baroque music. As in the case of *Antico Edition*, most of the issues contain a small group of pieces, for example, *Four chansons by Machaut* and *Six duets from the Renaissance*, though *Monophonic dances of the 14th century* offers thirteen. In varying sizes though roughly approximating to A4 paper these are practical editions, but some may find the absence of bar lines in many of the earlier pieces a problem.

Background reading

Munrow, David, *Instruments of the middle ages and renaissance*, Oxford University Press, 1976.

Two companion records EMI SLS 988.

Seay, Albert, *Music in the medieval world*, Prentice-Hall, Englewood Cliffs, New Jersey, U.S.A. 2nd edition, 1975.

Sternfeld, F. W. (ed.), *A history of Western music*, vol. 1: *Music from the middle ages to the renaissance*, Weidenfeld and Nicolson, 1973.

Sources

The music and original words of the songs are based on the transcriptions listed below although some of these have been modified and adapted for use in this book. Unless otherwise noted, English song words are by Brian Sargent.

1 Song: Naples, Bibl. Naz. VI E40. Transcription in G. Reese, *Music in the Renaissance*, adapted with the permission of W. W. Norton & Company, Inc. and J. M. Dent & Sons Ltd. Copyright 1954 by W. W. Norton & Company, Inc.
Consort version: Rome, Bibl. Casanatense 2856. Transcription in J. Marix, *Les musiciens de la cour de Bourgogne*, Éditions de l'Oiseau-Lyre, 1937. Also appears in B. Trowell (ed.), *Invitation to medieval music 3*, Stainer and Bell, 1976.

2 Oxford, Bodleian Library, Wood 591. Transcription in F. Ll. Harrison, *Music in medieval Britain*, Routledge and Kegan Paul, 1958.

3 Cambridge University Library, Additional MS 5943. Transcription by B. Sargent; also appears in L. S. Myers, *Music, cantelenas, songs etc. from an early fifteenth-century manuscript*, 1906. The transcription by Lindo Myers ignores the first note of the piece in the manuscript. I gratefully acknowledge the help of Richard Rastall with my transcription.

4 Paris, Bibl. Nat. fr. 22543, fo. 62b. Transcription in A. Davison and W. Apel, *Historical anthology of music*, vol. 1, Harvard University Press/Oxford University Press, new edition 1949. Also appears in H. Gleason, *Examples of music before 1400*, Appleton-Century-Crofts Inc., 1942, and elsewhere.

5 Melody and words from the *Mosburg Gradual*, 1360. Three-part version: Cambridge University Library, Ff.i.17, fo. 4v. Transcription in F. Ll. Harrison (ed.), *Now make we merthe*, book 1, Oxford University Press, 1968, and elsewhere.

6 Aosta MS. Seminario 4. Transcription in F. Ll. Harrison (ed.), *Now make we merthe*, book 1, Oxford University Press, 1968.

7 Cambridge University Library, Additional MS 5943. Transcription in L. S. Myers, *Music, cantelenas, songs etc. from an early fifteenth-century manuscript*, 1906. The modernized version of the text is by Brian Turner.

8 British Library MS Royal, Appendix 58 fo. 5. Transcription in J. Stevens, *Music and poetry in the early Tudor court*, Methuen, 1961.

9 British Library, Egerton MS 274. Transcription in D. Wulstan (ed.), *An anthology of carols*, Chester, 1968.

10 Berlin, Deutsche Bibl. 40098 (Z.89). Transcription in H. Ringmann, *Das Glogauer Liederbuch*, Bärenreiter, 1927.

11 Munich, Staatsbibliothek, Cod. germ. 4997: Kolmarer Liederhandschrift fo. 528r. Transcription in F. Gennrich, *Troubadours, Trouvères, Minnesang and Meistergesang*, Arno Volk Verlag, 1960.

12 and 13 Paris, Bibl. Nat. MS.f.frçs.1584 and others. Transcription in L. Schrade (ed.), *Polyphonic music of the fourteenth century*, vol. III, Éditions de l'Oiseau-Lyre, 1956. Also appears in F. Ludwig (ed.), *Guillaume de Machaut: Musikalische Werke*, vol. I, Breitkopf & Härtel, 1926; *Guillaume de Machaut: Oeuvres complètes*, vol. I, *Les virelais*, Édition commémorative établie par S. Leguy, Le Droict Chemin de Musique, Paris 1977, and elsewhere.

14 Madrid, Library of the Escorial, MS.j.b.2, fo. 159v. Transcription in A. Hughes (ed.), *New Oxford history of music*, vol. II, Oxford University Press, 1954.

15 Montserrat, *Llibre Vermell*, MS.1, fo. 26v. Transcription in G. Suñol, 'Els cants del Romeus', *Analecta montserratensia*, I (1917) 100. Also appears in K. Meyer-Baer, *Music of the spheres and the Dance of Death*, Princeton University Press, 1970, G. Reese, *Music in the middle ages*, Dent, 1941, and elsewhere.

16 Paris, Bibl. de l'Arsenal 5198. Transcription in F. Gennrich, *Troubadours, Trouvères, Minnesang and Meistergesang*, Arno Volk Verlag, 1960. Also appears in H. Gleason, *Examples of music before 1400*, Appleton-Century-Crofts, Inc., 1942.

17 Codex Montpellier, Fac. des Médecins H 196, fo. 234v. Transcription in A. Davison and W. Apel, *Historical anthology of music*, vol. I. Copyright Harvard University Press, 1949.

18 Wolfenbüttel, Herzog August Bibliothek MS 1206, fo. 197v.–198v. Words and music based on Hare, Hare, Hye! – Balaam from *A Medieval Motet Book* edited Hans Tischler. Copyright 1973 Associated Music Publishers, Inc., by permission of G. Schirmer Ltd., London.

19 Oxford, Bodleian Library, Canonici misc. 213, p. 62. Transcription in H. Besseler (ed.), *Guillaume Dufay: Opera omnia*, vol. V, American Institute of Musicology, 1966, by kind permission of Dr Carapetyan, Director, AIM. Also appears in a leaflet by M. Bukofzer, Mercury Music Corporation, 1949.

20 Florence, Bibl. Laurenziana, *Codex squarcialupi*, Pal. 87, 135r. Transcription in L. Schrade (ed.), *Polyphonic music of the fourteenth century*, vol. IV, Éditions de l'Oiseau-Lyre, 1958/1974. Also appears in L. Ellinwood, *The works of Francesco Landini*, Medieval Academy of America, 1945/1970.

21 Orléans, Bibl. de la Ville, MS 201, 205–214. Transcription in N. Greenberg and W. Smoldon (eds.), *The Play of Herod*, Oxford University Press, 1965. Also appears in W. Smoldon (ed.), *Herod*, Stainer & Bell, 1960, and elsewhere.

22 British Library, MS Harleian 978, fo. 2–4v. Transcription by B. Sargent. Also appears in H. V. Hughes (ed.), *Early English harmony*, vol. II, Plainsong and Mediaeval Music Society, 1913. I am grateful to Gilbert Reaney for advice in the transcription of this piece.

23 Oxford, Bodleian Library, Douce 381, fo. 23. Transcription in P. Marr (ed.), *Four medieval pieces*, Hinrichsen Edition, Peters Edition Ltd, London, 1972. Also appears in T. Dart, 'A new source of English organ music', *Music and Letters*, XXXV (1954) 201.

24 Petrucci, *Harmonice musices odhecaton A* (Venice, 1501). Transcription in T. Dart (ed.), *Invitation to medieval music*, vol. II, Stainer & Bell, 1969.

25 Regensburg, Bibl. Proske, MS A.R. 940/41. Transcription in W. Brennecke, *Carmina germanica et gallica*, vol. I, Bärenreiter, 1956.

Sources of illustrations

Front cover from the Cantiga de Santa Maria, Library of the Escorial, Madrid; **p.1** University Library, Heidelberg; **pp.4, 5** (below) Luttrell Psalter, British Library; **pp.5** (above), **9** School of Fine Arts, University of East Anglia; **p.6** Biblioteca Trivulziana, Milan Cod. 1025, fo. 142; **pp.11, 13** Bodleian Library, Oxford MS. Douce 93 fo. 28; **p.19** University of Illinois Press; photograph Cambridge University Library; **p.22** Bibliotheque Nationale, Paris MS. fr.1584 fo. E; **p.25** New York Public Library; photograph Cambridge University Library; **p.29** British Library, Egerton MS. 3307, fo. 72; **p.31** Bibliotheque Nationale, Paris MS. fr. 12.476; Photographie Giraudon; **p.32** Biblioteca Medicea Laurenziana, Florence. Codex Squarcialupi Palat. 87, c.121; **p.33** Bibliotheque Nationale, Paris MS. Fonds Rothschild 3010 56; **p.43** Reproduced by courtesy of the Trustees of the British Museum; **p.45** Bibliotheque Nationale, Paris MS.fr.12572 p.119.

For EU product safety concerns, contact us at Calle de José Abascal, 56–1º,
28003 Madrid, Spain or eugpsr@cambridge.org

www.ingramcontent.com/pod-product-compliance
Ingram Content Group UK Ltd.
Pitfield, Milton Keynes, MK11 3LW, UK
UKHW051918230326
469290UK00009B/159